NONE SHALL LACK THEIR MATE

Volume 1

By Dr. Hope McDowell-Gibson

HOPE ACROSS NATIONS
BRAMPTON, ONTARIO

Copyright © 2017 by Dr. Hope McDowell-Gibson
ISBN: 978-1-7750473-4-6

All rights reserved

No part of this publication may be reproduced or transmitted, in any form or by any means, electronic or mechanical, including photocopy, recording or by any information storage or retrieval system without the express, written permission of the author. For permission requests, write to the publisher, addressed "Attention: Permissions Coordinator," at the address below.

Dr. Hope McDowell-Gibson/Hope Across Nations
Brampton, ON Canada
info@hopeacrossnations.ca
www.hopeacrossnations.ca

Scripture taken from the Holy Bible, King James Version. Cambridge Edition: 1769; King James Bible Online, 2017. www.kingjamesbibleonline.org.

Scripture taken from t*he Holy Bible,* **The Message (MSG)** *version, Copyright © 1993, 2002, 2018 by Eugene H. Peterson, https://www.biblegateway.com*

Scriptures taken from the Holy Bible, New International Version®, NIV®. Copyright © 1973, 1978, 1984, 2011 by Biblica, Inc.™ Used by permission of Zondervan. All rights reserved worldwide. www.zondervan.com The "NIV" and "New International Version" are trademarks registered in the United States Patent and Trademark Office by Biblica, Inc.™

Dedication

To all Women of Virtue; in the Body of Christ, who have dedicated their lives to our Lord Jesus Christ.

Especially to Minister Shevonie Powell, who has inspired me to write this noble book of inspirational prayers, for single women who desire to be married.

TABLE OF CONTENTS

Forward	7
Introduction	9
Preparing To Become A Virtuous Wife	11
Possessing The Meek And Quite Spirit	27
Guarding Your Thoughts	31
Prayers For Deliverance	34
Breakthrough Prayers For Single Women Desiring To Be Married:	35
Testimonials	37
Hymn-To A Good Wife	39
About the Author	41

FORWARD

Many women have met their husbands and have a normal family life. Others have had failure. In a recent survey, it indicated that almost four million African American women can't find a husband. In the Church the large number of single women hoping to get married is at an alarming rate. So many have given up hope in this area and sad to say some have even fallen prey to same sex relationships, while others ended up having children out of wedlock.

Yet, so many Pastors are dancing around this crisis and I have even heard many single women saying that Jesus is their husband. But is there not a solution? Sure there is, as where the natural fails, then we must turn to the Supernatural.

Surely, with God nothing is IMPOSSIBLE. Recalled, when Isaac was ready to get married and Abraham sent out his servant to find a wife for him, at first he was worried that he would returned empty from his mission. However, Abraham dispelled his servant's doubt and said to him, "The Lord before I walked and served will [do a Supernatural Sign]. He will send His angel and prosper your way so that you will return with a wife for Isaac". Genesis 24:7 & 40.

Indeed, Supernaturally God connected Isaac to Rebecca. Even, in my own Ministry after praying for many singles both male and female; we have seen God Supernaturally connect relationships just like Isaac and Rebecca.

Her Excellency Rev Dr., The Honorable Hope McDowell-Gibson, OEA, in this volume; NONE SHALL LACK THEIR MATE, is pointing us to God's promise and His ability to bring it to pass if you dare to pray and believe. As it is written in scriptures, All of God promises are Yea and Amen, including this one, but we must receive when we pray and stop merely hoping or wishing for an answer.

She also pointed out the fact that if you truly received an answer to your prayers then demonstrates your faith by getting your wedding dress ready, start calling yourself a wife and so forth. Dr. Hope also emphasizes the importance of Character Preparation in developing that "Meek and Quiet Spirit" that the Bible says, in the sight of God, a GREAT PRICE. Cultivate, also the inward beauty even more than the outward.

I can truly testify that the recommendations in this volume work. We have the proof in our congregation at No Limits Ministries International.

Therefore, I highly recommend this book not only to Singles but to the Married Couples as well.

H.E. Right Rev Dr. The Hon Phillip S Phinn, OEA, D-CPC
Presiding Bishop of No Limits Ministries International
Brampton/Toronto Canada

INTRODUCTION

This book is written out of a deep concern as to why there are so many devoted Christian Women in the church who have been single for years.

As a pastor, I have the responsibility of counseling, encouraging, mentoring, guiding and praying for God to keep them faithful to Him while they wait.
None Shall Lack Their Mate book is a series that will prepare single women to become virtuous wives.

In addition to this, other series will answer the big question that so many may have. Which is; "Now that I am married what next? This series we will uncover truths about how to maintain a good marriage so that couples will remain happily married.

The prayer points listed on page 35 of the book are scriptural and strategic in getting answers to prayers quickly. Pray in faith believing that "you shall have what you say". (Mark 11:23 paraphrased)

Equally, praying in the Holy Spirit's language (tongues) after the prayer points allow you to birth your prayers into manifestation quickly. It is no wonder why we are encouraged in Ephesians 6:18 to pray always in the Spirit.

Sadly, this is a weapon that so many believers have neglected to use making their warfare much more difficult. There are many Christian women who are married today just by praying these prayer points.

Preparing To Become a Virtuous Wife

There are so many Christian women complaining of being single. They desperately want to get married but still haven't been able to get married. Undoubtedly, many of them are praying to God for years yet still no answer. What seem to be the problem?

As a pastor, this is a major concern since marriage was the first institution that God gave to mankind. In fact, the Lord said that it was not good for man to be alone.

As you read this book, None Shall Lack Their Mate; I hope it will provide keys to women who are waiting and preparing to be married.

I have had the privilege of mentoring and guiding many women to realize their dreams of becoming a virtuous wife.

The prayer points are scriptural and strategic therefore as you pray them in faith believing, I pray that you will be married quickly.

The Bible said, in Isaiah 34:16, not one shall lack her mate, for your mouth has commanded it, and your Spirit has gathered them.

This passage of scripture clearly shows that it is God's desire for everyone to be married except He grants a special grace to remain single for a particular assignment. This is mentioned in 1 Corinthians 7:7 about Apostle Paul's gift of celibacy.

Sometimes I wish everyone were single like me—a simpler life in many ways! But celibacy is not for everyone any more than marriage is. God gives the gift of the single life to some, the gift of the married life to others. (MSG) Albeit, in Hebrews 13:4 the Bible says: Let marriage be held in honour among all, and let the marriage bed be undefiled, for God will judge the sexually immoral and adulterous.
Marriage is honorable not only by a few, but among all. It is instituted by God to bring honour to your life. The whole man – spirit, soul, and body.

So if you desire a loving and godly spouse, it's okay to have such desires. God gave you that desire because He has someone special just for you.

You may not know how long it will take for your spouse to find you but he is somewhere out there. It is the Lord that will bring you together at the right time.

The Bible explains that; He who finds a wife finds a good thing and obtains favor from the Lord. (Proverbs 18:22 ESV)

Notice that it is the man that does the seeking, and as a result he finds. For this reason, women of virtue please allow a man to approach you.

While you are waiting, use this time to be alone with God, and enjoy these precious moments. These are days in which you have the opportunity to draw closer to God; developing an intimate relationship with Him. Capitalize on the fact that you are single and have this time to be alone with God in the secret place; take advantage of it.

As you grow closer to the Lord and hide his Word in your heart, your life will be transformed and also those around you. Especially, your husband and children will benefit from the fruit of the Spirit that is produced in your life according to Galatians 5:22-23.

In fact Apostle Paul commends single women, in 1 Corinthians 7:32-35 by saying;

I want you to live as free of complications as possible. When you're unmarried, you're free to concentrate on simply pleasing the Master. Marriage involves you in all the nuts and bolts of domestic life and in wanting to please your spouse, leading to so many more demands on your attention. The time and energy that married people spend on caring for and nurturing each other, the unmarried can spend in becoming whole and holy instruments of God. I'm trying to be helpful and make it as easy as possible for you, not make things harder. All I want is for you to be able to develop a way of life in which you can spend plenty of time together with the Master without a lot of distractions. (The Message (MSG) translation)

Essentially, what I am saying is to enjoy every season of your life. While you are single and waiting to be married don't be anxious or miserable but be happy. After you are married you will soon discover the joy of your past singleness; when you served the Lord without the distractions of wifely responsibilities. I am not at all suggesting that being married is not a happy stage of your life.

Absolutely, it is wonderful to share your life with the one you love but understand that marriage is not easy because true love is more than a feeling; it's a choice.

If you want your marriage to be strong and lasting, you must choose every day to love your spouse, whether you are feeling like it or not. If you choose to do this, your marriage will be one of the most fulfilling, gratifying and fruitful parts of your life.

Emotions are temporary; which means they are subjective to change. They come and go based on our state of mind. Anyone who is married can attest to this fact, that the feeling of love comes and goes.

Jesus modelled this kind of love for us in his sacrifice on the cross where he was stripped of everything yet he humbled himself by taking on the form of a man, coming down from heaven to earth to die for us. He chose to give up his life so that all who believe in him could have life.

Jesus' sacrifice was out of his great love for us. There is no greater love than to lay down your life for another. In the same way, in a marriage couples would lay down their lives for one another–giving of themselves to each other in the same way that Jesus gave his life for you.

Evidently, the virtuous woman must bring a humble heart and a submissive spirit to her marriage. Every day, you will need to choose to love your spouse by putting his desires ahead of your own. This kind of love is explained in detail in 1 Corinthians 13.

Consider this; Apostle Paul also spoke concerning the married life in 1 Corinthians 7:1-3 saying; now for the matters you wrote about: "It is good for a man not to have sexual relations with a woman." 2 But since sexual immorality is occurring, each man should have sexual relations with his own wife, and each woman with her own husband.

Understand that your role as a wife and help meet is to assist your godly Man of God to fulfill his destiny assignments. In light of this, there are some compelling questions that need to be answered. Such as, "Lord where do I need to grow in my heart to receive my husband?"

"Am I mature enough to handle the Man of God that you have for me?"

Evidence in support of this position, "help meet" can be found in; Genesis 2:18 where God said, "It's not good for the Man to be alone; I'll make him a helper, a companion."

Imagine, Jesus referred to the Holy Spirit as a "Helper", the Greek wordveiled parman meaning aid.
In the same way, God used the title helper to describe the wife's role who, like the Holy Spirit has been called to help her husband.

This title, "Helper" is not used to belittle or undermine a woman in anyway; but to show her strength. She comes alongside her husband because alone, he is not sufficient (it's not good for him to be alone) in carrying out his assignments.

It is important to note though, that communication is key when helping your spouse with his assignments. As he needs to share his visions and in whatever capacity help is needed.

I am reminded years ago when I had just gotten married, it was such a joy and a delight to go home after work; to prepare dinner and serve my husband. Today, it is still such a pleasure to serve him and go out and do errands that make his life much easier.

Women of God, we are the helper that men need, not in a subservient way, but because of their inadequacy.

Considering this, we can now see why marriage is a union designed by God where the two become one. In other words, a woman complements the man. This is a position of dignity and not of dishonor.

With this understanding of God's perspectives on marriage; applying them to your life. Certainly, you will have a rewarding and fulfilling marriage.

Women it's indeed an honour and privilege to carry the title "Helper" as the Holy Spirit. (John 14:16 & 26) This shows our strength and significance!

    Furthermore, it's the role of the virtuous wife to provide practically, spiritually and emotionally support to her husband as she cares for him and her household every day.

    By the same token, she must choose to give life to her family and be one who offers them comfort and caregiving. As a homemaker she also has the responsibility of making the home a safe haven for her husband. Likewise, she is also a positive influence for her children so that they will benefit from her training and guidance.

Proverbs 19:14 (b) explains that a prudent wife is from the Lord.

Notice, becoming a prudent wife, results out of a relationship from the Lord; as you submit yourself to Him. He leads you to wisdom and understanding.

So what does it mean to be prudent? The dictionary defines prudent as:

1. Careful or wise in handling practical matters; exercising good judgment or common sense: a prudent manager of money.

2. Characterized by or resulting from care or wisdom in practical matters or in planning for the future. To be shrewd, in home management.

Based on the definition above we can therefore, use these seven words to describe the prudent wife:
- Godly Woman
- Wise
- Understanding
- Intelligent
- Insightful
- Good Steward
- Shrewd

The question is, are you demonstrating these qualities as you prepare yourself to be that prudent wife?

Paradoxically, marriage is not about what I can get from my husband but how can I help him to get to where he needs to go. It's about giving of yourself to please your spouse, as you are united as one; knowing that his success is your success as well.

The popular quote still holds true; "behind every successful man there is a strong woman".

The amazing love story in the bible about Ruth and Boaz shows how she displayed selflessness in serving her ex-mother in law Naomi. This results in her meeting her Man of God who later became her, kinsman redeemer. Ruth, a Moabite (they were an evil nation and enemies of Israel) sought after God and made the difficult decision to follow God. She chose to leave Moab, and clung to Naomi. She also made a choice to glean and not to complain or ask for handouts in order to support herself and Naomi.

Ruth was obedient in following Naomi's instructions to approach Boaz. If she had not served Naomi she would have missed her blessings.

The first time Boaz spoke with Ruth he commended her for her unselfish act of kindness expressed to her mother-in-law, Naomi. Boaz said this to her, "I've been told all about what you have done for your mother-in-law since the death of your husband—how you left your father and mother and your homeland and came to live with a people you did not know before. (Ruth 2:11) NIV

Boaz later became the kinsman-redeemer and husband for Ruth. He also provided protection for her; based on the fact that her reputation had preceded her.

For this reason; he said, "You are a woman of noble character".
Women of virtue it is important to bring your invaluable gift of character in your marriage. This will speak volume for you.

In the same manner, Ruth willingly served Naomi, so must women be ready to serve their husbands and not entering into marriage to be served.

Jesus shared the same sentiments, in Matthew 20:28, by saying "the Son of Man came not to be served, but to serve. Giving this mind set, your marriage will be fulfilling and a lasting one.

She moved from being a Moabite to be listed in the generation of Jesus Christ. So, Ruth marries Boaz and they produce a son Obed, who then had Jesse, and Jesse had David. We learnt from scripture that Jesus was from the lineage of David.

The interesting story in Ruth chapter 2, how she got favoured from the man who marries her, because she serves

Naomi her mother in law. Woman of Virtue, sow seed of kindness into others it will germinate.

Truthfully, you can serve your way into marriage; the question is who are you serving? I once mentored a young woman a few years ago; my charge to her was to serve her way into marriage. She obeyed the instructions and is married today.

This is clearly seen in Ruth chapter 3:8 where at midnight Boaz discovered Ruth laying at his feet. She found favour with Boaz and he called her a virtuous woman.

If you desire to find your godly spouse quickly, I encourage you to follow the examples of Ruth. Midnight is the third watch of the night to engage in strategic prayers and intercession for your Man of God to locate you in the realm of the spirit. See prayer points listed on page 35. Then he will be manifested in the physical.

I once counselled a young woman from my ministry who has never been married and she was very concerned at that time. So I told her that for the next six months she should declare; "I AM A WIFE". Within six months she came back to me asking for pre-marital counselling; today she is happily married.

Similarly, we see another love story of Esther who prepared herself for one year before her wedding. This

helps her to understand how to operate in the palace. Yet we see many giving themselves into marriage ill-advisedly by totally disregarding the need for pre-marital counselling. It takes wisdom to build a house and understanding to set it on a firm foundation; it takes knowledge to furnish its rooms with fine furniture and beautiful draperies.
Proverbs 24:3-4

The King loved Esther more than all the other women and she obtained grace and favor in his sight more than all the virgins; so the King set the royal crown upon her head and made her queen instead of Vashti. That's Divine Replacement! The King made a decree For All wives to honour their husbands, both great and small.

In Esther 2:17, Vashti was removed, because of a spirit of "Rebellion" where she disrespected her husband, the King publicly. While Esther, was chosen instead because of her humility.

A Pastor once came to me crying; because his wife was so abusive and he said; "Prophetess many Men of God in the pulpit are bleeding because their wives have become rebellious". Women, God want us to honour our husbands as priests. We can learn valuable lessons from Sarah who called her husband, Abraham lord out of reverence and godly fear. Lordship means to revere or respect someone highly by obeying them.

Ephesians 5:33 explains saying; each one of you also must love his wife as he loves himself, and the wife must respect her husband.

The husband however has a greater responsibility to love his wife as Christ loves the church and gave himself for it.

Emerson Eggerichs, the best-selling author of Love and Respect, states; "Women need love. Men need respect. This is a simply fact that so many women are ignorant of. He further explains, "What we have missed is the husband's need for respect and how the wife can fulfill her need to be loved by giving her husband what he needs—respect".

He also affirms that, "Husbands are made to be respected, want respect, and expect respect.

Many wives have the notion that if they can just love their husbands more then they will in turn show them more love.

On the contrary, when a wife respects and submits to her husband, he naturally responds in love to her. In the same way Christ loves the church and gave himself for it. Likewise, when she is loved and cared for by her husband she naturally respects him as well.

This is how God designed husband and wife relationship. Consider this; men are wired to receive respect. Yet, so many wives fail to show this.

As a certified Marriage Officer, whenever I counsel couples who are getting married, the area of respect is usually covered in detail during the pre-marital sessions. Most of the marriages that result in divorce is because of constant disrespect shown to husbands. This eventually causes a breakdown in the marriage. Respect can be communicated through verbal and non-verbal behaviors; this is especially important when there are disagreements. We can therefore, learn valuable lessons from Vashti's fate in the book of Esther Chapter 1:12-20. It was a serious breach in the marriage, so much so, that the King published a decree throughout His Kingdom.

"So, if the King agrees, let him pronounce a royal ruling and have it recorded in the laws of the Persians and Medes so that it cannot be revoked, that Vashti is permanently banned from King Xerxes' presence. And then let the King give her royal position to a woman who knows her place. When the King's ruling becomes public knowledge throughout the kingdom, extensive as it is, every woman, regardless of her social position, will show proper respect to her husband." Esther 1:19-20 MSG

It is therefore noteworthy; to call forth your husband at midnight that there shall be a Divine Replacement in case there is a "Vashti" that is occupying him.

I declare; that as you read this book you shall receive your King. Any Vashti (a woman that is dishonouring her man) that's holding up your King will be removed in Jesus Name.

As aforementioned, Esther's preparation took twelve months; this entails beautifying herself with oils and precious fragrance.

Like Ruth served Naomi, Esther served Mordecai, her uncle.

This signifies that becoming a wife is a process. It takes working on yourself; God will not do it for you. But as you submit to Him in prayer and consecration He will deliver you from anything that as hinder you from getting married.

Inner healing is also very important on your journey of becoming a wife. This will help to remove all unresolved issues of the past.

It's important to note that, reflecting the fruit of the Spirit that's demonstrated in love and Christ-Like Character.

There is an aura or fragrance that every believer should possess that will attract the right friends or spouse to them. A simple smile shows an individual state of well-being.

POSSESSING THE MEEK AND QUIET SPIRIT

1 Peter 3:3-4 admonishes women to focus on beautifying their hearts; so they shine from inside out. Rather than spending so much time beautifying themselves outwardly.

It reads...
3 "Do not let your adornment be merely outward-arranging the hair, wearing gold, or putting on fine apparel
4 rather let it be the hidden person of the heart, with the incorruptible beauty of a meek and quiet spirit, which is very precious in the sight of God."

Surprisingly, so many women spend so much time on makeup, grooming the hair and wearing flashy and expensive clothing which is outward beautification. Yet, neglecting the inward appearance, the hidden man, which is the heart. The scripture clearly explains that the inward person (heart) is the real person that needs to be renewed daily by using the word of God through meditation.

Obviously, the outward man can be a facade as so many women are well dressed on the outside while there is so much hurt or pretense in the heart.
It is no wonder why many of the problems people are experiencing today, particularly married couples, this is as

a result of neglecting the inward appearance while too much emphasis is placed on their outward appearance.

A few years ago as I was carefully doing my makeup making sure it was flawless; when the Holy Spirit spoke clearly to me saying; "the heart of the matter is the heart; the same way you spend time to adorn yourself; spend much more time to adorn your heart".

Indeed, this was an instruction that I will never forget to heed. As a result, I divert most of my attention to feeding my spirit man with Prayer and the Word of God. Then I began to carry the presence and atmosphere of the Holy Spirit that attracted good things in my life.

We are reminded in Psalm 149:4 That the Lord takes pleasure in His people and He will beautify the meek with salvation.

It is often said that beauty is on the inside. True beauty doesn't come from the makeup we put on, but rather true beauty comes from the heart. When we are beautiful on the inside, it will reflect on the outside.
How is beauty characterized in this passage of scripture?

Beauty in this context is defined as possessing different qualities such as gentleness, meekness, humility, grace, joy, self-control, patience, truthfulness, kindness, happiness, and loyalty that can shine through a person, making them a positive example for everyone around them.

All of these are expressions of love.
These attributes don't just happen but must be cultivated and developed by the Holy Spirit in you.

Sadly, there is a breakdown in relationships and families that has affected so many different areas such as the home, church and the wider society. Could this be traced to the fact that most women focus 90% of their time on adorning the physical appearance rather than; who they are on the inside?

What about our Christian values of standing for righteous living and refusing to compromise.

Is there anything wrong with hair do's and dressing up in nice clothing and jewelry? Certainly not! However, if too much attention and focus is made on the outward appearance, then we maybe neglecting to feed the spirit man with the Word of God. According to Proverbs 31, the woman to be admired and praised is the woman who lives in the Fear-of-God.

Wives, notice I am addressing you as wives because the Bible said, in Proverbs 18:22; he who finds a wife; this means you must become and demonstrate wifely qualities in order for your husband to find or discover you. The godly Man of God is not just looking for a woman, but a woman who produces wifely qualities and behaviors.

I therefore, admonish you to study how to become a virtuous wife by reading and meditating Proverbs 31:10-31.

In my next series I will be covering the Virtuous Wife; see Hymn, To A Good Wife on page 39.

GUARDING YOUR THOUGHTS

"As he thinks in his heart, so is he" (Proverbs 23:7). This means, whatever you meditate you become so your thoughts shape the person you are.

It is no surprise that most problems that people are facing results from wrong thinking. This passage of scripture provides powerful truths in keeping watch over what we allow to get in our hearts. Simply, don't allow negative thoughts to get in your heart, stop it by reflecting on truths from the Word of God.

"Keep your heart with all diligence, for out of it spring the issues of life" (Proverbs 4:23).
Apostle Paul gives us a guideline for right thinking in Philippians 4:8;
"Whatever things are true ... noble ... just ... pure ... lovely ... of good report ... meditate on these things"

It is important to practice meditating the Word in order to have right thinking, because whenever you are meditating on the scriptures your mind is occupied with right thoughts. The scriptures will also give you a positive mindset that will guide your life in the right direction.

The wrong kind of thinking can block you from becoming that virtuous wife. The devil will tempt you with thoughts like, "I will never be married," "I am too old so nobody will marry me", "I was hurt in the past so I will be hurt again," "He must be tall and handsome otherwise I am not going be married," "I have my ministry so if he is not in ministry I cannot marry him", or, "I am not good enough."

This kind of thinking will sow seeds of unbelief and doubt that will delay your breakthrough in getting married. Your thoughts ultimately govern your actions.

Faith is the Key

Start making plans for your wedding, do simple things like buying your bridal gown. The idea of seeing is believing holds true; as you do Prayers of Thanksgiving looking at that bridal gown will give a sense of victory in your spirit that is done.

Interestingly, some women will hang a man's shirt in their closet as this help to build their faith. Avoid seeing, saying, reading, or hearing anything that suggests loneliness.

Remember, if you can see your husband through the eyes of your faith, then you shall have him. The Lord asked Jeremiah, the Prophet; "what do you see?" Based on Jeremiah's response He said, I will hasten my word to perform it. (Jeremiah 1:11 & 12)

What you see is what you perceive, what you perceive is what you conceive and what you conceive is what you will ultimately receive. Can you see your Man of God proposing to you? Or can you see yourself married and serving him? Then begin to thank God that "I AM A WIFE! God said, NOW! I will hasten my words to perform it.

PRAY THESE PRAYER POINTS

PRAYERS FOR DELIVERANCE

Finally, perhaps these are past relationships that we must rid our souls of; it's a spiritual connection than it is a physical one.

Let's renounce all ungodly soul ties from previous relationships. Also forgive anyone who has hurt or rejected you in the past. Know this, forgiveness is the gateway to your freedom in order to love again also for your breakthrough in other areas of your life.

I renounce any rebellious spirit in the name of Jesus.

I renounce any generational curse that has affected my family blood line or the women in my family. Lord let your blood purge my family bloodline.

I denounce any spirit husband that has attached themselves to me, in the name of Jesus….

I renounce all ungodly soul ties from all relationships in my past

I forgive anyone who has hurt, rejected or abuse me, in the name of Jesus

Anything in my past that's hindering my future, I renounce it, in the name of Jesus.

Any word curse that was spoken against my life by myself or anyone, that's hindering me from getting married, or staying married I break it in the name of Jesus.

BREAKTHROUGH PRAYERS FOR SINGLE WOMEN DESIRING TO BE MARRIED

The Bible said, in Isaiah 34:16 none shall lack their mate. For your mouth has commanded it, and your spirit has gathered them. (paraphrase)

O Lord right now, let your Spirit gather my mate. Let your Angels locate him now in the name of Jesus!

I shall not lack my mate in the name of Jesus!

Any spirit that's hindering or delaying me from getting married I interrupt it in the name of Jesus

Lord according to your word; I am a wife and a joyful mother of children

I declare that I AM a wife!

As a wife I am like a fruitful vine by the sides of my house.

I am a virtuous woman, a Proverbs 31 Woman.

I am a woman that fears the Lord therefore, I shall be celebrated

I am a help meet to my Man of God so that he will carry out his God-Given destiny assignments

Lord I declare that my husband will love and cherish me like Christ love His Bride, the Church.

Lord birth in me a meek and quiet spirit so that I will be able to submit to my husband

Lord let the Grace that was on Esther's life come upon me in the name of Jesus

Lord as Esther was anointed with special fragrance and oil to attract her King and position in the palace. So will I be anointed with the oil of joy for inner beauty and favor

Any Vashti that's occupying my husband Must be release now in the name of Jesus

Lord you shall beautify the meek with salvation therefore, let your glory shine upon me. Lord beautify me with your salvation

I enter the realm of the spirit and take dominion over the spirit of singleness and barrenness

I declare love doors, marriage doors and happiness doors be open now in Jesus Name... Be Open, Open, Open!

By faith I call forth my godly husband in Jesus Name, wherever you are, you must locate me.

Thank you Mighty God for sending your angels on assignment to bring my breakthrough

    Prayer Points Continued....

Pray with Prophetess Hope on YouTube: See video address below.

https://youtu.be/N_Nn0cTm3JU

Testimonials

Marriage Testimonials:

A few years ago Prophetess Hope mentored me in preparing to be a virtuous wife. She encouraged me to serve my way into marriage. I started serving in different capacity in the church. Later, my husband met me serving with her at a House Prayer Meeting. Like, Boaz my husband commended me for serving the Woman of God.
Thanking God for Prophetess Hope, keep preparing and mentoring women to become virtuous wives.
Mrs Shernette Esdaille

Recently, I was very broken because my dad was ill and I was also concerned about the fact that I was single and has never been married. So I went to Prophetess Hope who is still my Pastor today. She counselled me and told me that for the next six months I am to declare that "I AM a WIFE".

Yes, I am now a wife because of the help and prayer that was given to me by Prophetess Hope. She instructed me to pray a specific prayer for 6 months and I did and shortly after I went to visit my dad in Jamaica I met my husband.
Praise Jesus I am now *Mrs. Andrea Goulbourne-Lawson.*

In 2016 while we we're driving to Eaton Centre; Pastor Hope had a vision of me walking down the aisle in a long bridal dress.

However, she saw that it was a Man of God but couldn't see his face.

Later, in 2018 while I was being mentored and counselled by Pastor Hope who is also my spiritual mother. She prophesied that I am an "Esther"; and I was to be very prayerful over the next 60 days.

As I obeyed in daily Prayer and Intercession; in less than 60 days I went to a grocery store to shop. Unexpectedly, I was approached by a gentleman who asked my name and if he could speak with me.

Nonchalantly, I replied, Esther; and asked him to wait; then continued to shop. Unbelievably, this young man, stood there still waiting on me. This Man of God is my husband today and he later testified how shocked he was that my name was Esther. Since, he had been crying to God to send him his "Esther".

Thank you, Pastor for encouraging me to be that Esther that God has called me to be.

Mrs. Alisha "Esther" Warren-Lalor

Hymn - To a Good Wife

A good woman is hard to find,
    and worth far more than diamonds.
Her husband trusts her without reserve,
    and never has reason to regret it.
Never spiteful, she treats him generously
    all her life long.
She shops around for the best yarns and cottons,
    and enjoys knitting and sewing.
She's like a trading ship that sails to faraway places
    and brings back exotic surprises.
She's up before dawn, preparing breakfast
    for her family and organizing her day.
She looks over a field and buys it,
    then, with money she's put aside, plants a garden.
First thing in the morning, she dresses for work,
    rolls up her sleeves, eager to get started.
She senses the worth of her work,
    is in no hurry to call it quits for the day.
She's skilled in the crafts of home and hearth,
    diligent in homemaking.
She's quick to assist anyone in need,
    reaches out to help the poor.
She doesn't worry about her family when it snows;
    their winter clothes are all mended and ready to wear.
She makes her own clothing,
    and dresses in colorful linens and silks.
Her husband is greatly respected
    when he deliberates with the city fathers.

She designs gowns and sells them,
   brings the sweaters she knits to the dress shops.
Her clothes are well-made and elegant,
   and she always faces tomorrow with a smile.
When she speaks she has something worthwhile to say,
   and she always says it kindly.
She keeps an eye on everyone in her household,
   and keeps them all busy and productive.
Her children respect and bless her;
   her husband joins in with words of praise:
"Many women have done wonderful things,
   but you've outclassed them all!"
Charm can mislead and beauty soon fades.
   The woman to be admired and praised
   is the woman who lives in the Fear-of-God.
Give her everything she deserves!
   Festoon her life with praises!

Proverbs 31:10-31 The Message (MSG)

ABOUT THE AUTHOR

Her Excellency Rev Dr. the Honorable Hope McDowell-Gibson, OEA, Th.D., Ph.D. Prophetess, Senior Pastor, Co-Founder of No Limits Ministries International, and Ambassador to Canada for A United Nations Accredited International organizations [WOLMI], Vice Chancellor for CICA International University & Seminary.

Dr. Hope has purposed to encouraged and provide development of creative Leadership to the Body of Christ.

Most Recently Dr. Hope was promoted as WOLMI Chief Ambassador to the United Nations Headquarters in Geneva. Switzerland and was Commissioned as Commander of the Most Distinguished Order of Extraordinary Ambassadors.

She is the Author of THE PERSON OF THE HOLY SPIRIT IN YOU.

Ambassador Dr. Hope McDowell-Gibson is the Wife of Terrence Gibson and the Mother of Zoe and Nathan Gibson, residing in Brampton/Toronto Canada.

www.ingramcontent.com/pod-product-compliance
Lightning Source LLC
Chambersburg PA
CBHW071803040426
42446CB00012B/2684